Xtreme Athletes
Michael Phelps

Xtreme Athletes

Michael Phelps

Kerrily Sapet

MORGAN REYNOLDS

PUBLISHING

Greensboro, North Carolina

Xtreme Athletes

Michael Phelps
David Beckham
Danica Patrick
Kelly Slater
Shaun White

XTREME ATHLETES: MICHAEL PHELPS

Copyright © 2009 by Kerrily Sapet

Library of Congress Cataloging-in-Publication Data

Sapet, Kerrily, 1972-
  Xtreme athletes : Michael Phelps / by Kerrily Sapet.
    p. cm.
  Includes bibliographical references and index.
  ISBN 978-1-59935-077-6
  1. Phelps, Michael, 1985- 2. Swimmers--United States--Biography. I.
Title.
GV838.P54S37 2007
797.2'1092--dc22
[B]

                                    2007041505

Printed in the United States of America

First Edition

To my grandmothers, with love

Contents

Michael Phelps
(Courtesy of Matthew Stockman/Getty Images)

one

Born to Swim

While the other kids in the swimming class bobbed up and down and practiced floating, seven-year-old Michael Phelps refused to put his face under water and tried to sneak out of the pool.

"I'm cold. I have to go to the bathroom. Maybe if I just sit on the side and watch the other kids do it," he whined to his teacher.

He scowled and kicked when she plunged him into the water anyway. She bribed him with a candy bar and started him off with the backstroke, so he couldn't see the water underneath him. Soon Michael learned to float and to move his arms and legs without sinking. Within weeks his mother and teacher had

more trouble getting him out of the water than they'd had getting him in. But no one would guess that one day swimming fans around the world would call this skinny boy the Human Shark, as he blasted away world records and won gold medals.

Michael Fred Phelps II was born in Baltimore, Maryland on June 30, 1985. His parents, Fred and Debbie, had two other children, seven-year-old Hilary and five-year-old Whitney. Even though Fred and Debbie grew up in small towns where boys played football and girls cheered at their games, all three of the Phelps children would one day become competitive swimmers.

Fred Phelps grew up in a remote valley in the Appalachian Mountains, where the Potomac River separates Maryland and West Virginia. In Luke, Fred's hometown, three seasons marked the year: hunting, fishing, and football. It was a tight-knit community where people sealed business deals with a handshake and didn't lock their doors.

"They don't care about keeping up with the Joneses," Fred Phelps said. "They don't know who the Joneses are."

Fred's father died suddenly from a blood clot when Fred was eight years old. He threw himself into sports, playing football, basketball, and baseball.

As a teenager at Bruce High School he met Debbie Davisson, who lived a few miles north in Westernport. By 1968, their senior year, they were dating seriously.

Throughout the 1960s Fred and Debbie watched as people from Luke and Westernport left for cities in search of better jobs. As Appalachian mill towns like theirs drained, those people remaining scrambled for stable employment and found it in classrooms. Both Debbie and Fred attended Fairmont State College in West Virginia, where they studied education and earned teaching certificates. They married in 1973. Soon after, Debbie found a job teaching home economics in Havre de Grace, Maryland, near Baltimore. Then, after a year of substitute teaching, Fred applied for a position with the Maryland state police. When he graduated from the police academy he began working as a state trooper.

In 1978, the couple's first daughter, Hilary, was born. Two years later they had a second daughter, Whitney. The Phelps's bought five acres of land in Whiteford, Maryland, near the Pennsylvania line. A stream flowed behind their peaceful property and deer flitted through the woods. But the harmony didn't last long, and Debbie and Fred separated for a short time. In 1985, after they reunited, their third child, Michael, was born.

On a pediatrician's advice Debbie signed her daughters up for swimming lessons. Both girls became excellent swimmers and began winning trophies at competitions. The only girls who bettered them practiced year-round. When Michael was three years old his family joined the North Baltimore Athletic Club, or NBAC. The club's serious swimmers trained at Meadowbrook pool, a seventy-mile roundtrip drive from the Phelps's' home, mainly on winding country roads. The family's world began to revolve around the girls' life in the pool.

Both Hilary and Whitney woke at four in the morning for swimming practices. In the chilly morning air, Debbie bundled young Michael in and out of the car for his sisters' practices and meets. His first memory was of the house's long driveway, and in warmer weather he toddled around the pool's picnic grove, zooming his toy cars under tables and mooching handouts from picnickers.

Debbie and Fred Phelps divided their days between working and shuttling their daughters to swimming. The tough schedule added more strain to their marriage. The little free time they had, they didn't spend together. Fred liked the country lifestyle in Whiteford and planted a large garden filled with tomatoes, corn, beans, and melons. Debbie enjoyed the suburbs and

The skyline of Baltimore, Maryland. Michael and his sisters trained at the Meadowbrook pool in north Baltimore.

wanted a shorter commute to Meadowbrook. In 1990, when Michael was five, the family moved to Towson, Maryland, a fifteen-minute drive to the pool.

Michael watched his sisters practice hard, but he also noticed they had fun with their swimming friends. After his first lessons, Michael begged his mother to go to the pool too and battled her when it was time to leave. But that same summer he broke his collarbone wrestling with a friend and had to wear a thick brace on his back. During the long hot summer Michael could only watch his friends splashing in the

cool water. When the brace came off that fall, he was itching to swim.

Soon Michael began swimming with the NBAC too. He loved the water and enjoyed the competitive games during practice. He especially liked when his coach named a category, such as ice cream flavors, and Michael could race against the person who named the same flavor he had. As Michael began to compete he started building a collection of ribbons. After finishing a one-mile swim in the Chesapeake Bay he told his mother that his future would involve swimming.

For Michael and his sisters the pool offered a haven from their parents' bickering. When Michael was eight years old Fred and Debbie Phelps divorced. Michael became friends with Matt Townsend, whose father had passed away.

The Chesapeake Bay Bridge in Maryland

Both Hilary and Whitney also helped their little brother through the rocky time. While their mother was at work, Hilary watched over him and Whitney became one of his best friends. Each morning Whitney woke Michael up after her practice and cooked him an egg sandwich for breakfast. The two piled anything they could find onto the sandwich, including cinnamon and peppers, and then Michael smothered it with heaps of mayonnaise. Whitney invented a Michael Sandwich, made of two slices of bread, with butter and jelly on both sides, two eggs, four slices of bacon, and one slice of cheese. Whitney packed Michael's lunch and walked him to the school bus.

Michael supported his sisters too. He cheered at their meets and painted his face, chest, and nose with the team's colors—red, yellow, and black. Sometimes the paint took days to wash off; other times it dyed his shirts in the wash.

Hilary became a strong distance swimmer, but Whitney went even further. In 1996, she swam the 200-meter butterfly faster than any other American woman, giving her a chance to go to the Olympics that year in Atlanta, Georgia. At the Olympic Trials Whitney faced enormous pressure. She was struggling with bulimia, an eating disorder common among female athletes, and a stress fracture in her back,

which sometimes made her arms and legs numb. Although she was in pain, she didn't complain, not wanting to jeopardize her chance to compete.

Eleven-year-old Michael watched as his sister didn't qualify for the Olympics, a keen disappointment for every family member. Although it helped Whitney realize she needed to care for her body, the loss fueled Michael's resolve to swim faster and better. He had listened to Whitney's stories and soaked in the details of her recent competition in Italy. An excellent swimmer in his own right, Michael already held national age group records and was known for winning five out of six events in one meet. Michael swam every day and at night dreamed of swimming, sometimes waking the family when he yelled "One, two, three . . . go!" in his sleep.

Swimming, along with the soccer, lacrosse, and baseball he played, did little to drain Michael's energy. He was constantly on the move, whether twirling salt shakers at the dinner table or sneaking up on people at the pool, tapping their shoulder, and running. The coaches frequently benched him for not listening during practices, making him sit by the lifeguard stand and remain silent for fifteen minutes.

Michael's teachers at Rodgers Forge Elementary School also noted his behavior. He was impulsive and inattentive. He and his friends sometimes sat in the back of class practicing signing autographs, hoping to become famous one day, but rarely paid attention to class and their teachers. One teacher commented that Michael would never be able to "focus on anything in his life." By sixth grade doctors diagnosed him with Attention Deficit Hyperactivity Disorder, or ADHD, which causes hyperactivity and difficulty paying attention. Fortunately Michael didn't have any of the other symptoms, such as depression or dyslexia. Doctors prescribed Ritalin, a drug for controlling the disorder, which Michael took three times a day to help calm him.

But Michael didn't take his medicine on weekends, and it showed. The young swimmers stood on kickboards in lines as they waited to swim their events. Anxious to swim, Michael often sneaked up to the front row, leaving his kickboard empty five or six spaces back. Parents and officials had to place him back in line. Other times Michael ran off to play. He reacted to his rare losses with emotional eruptions that frequently spiraled into goggle-throwing tantrums.

These outbursts stopped on the day Michael faced national competition and the other best swimmer in his age group. Michael lost, and wanted to heave his goggles across the pool. Instead he let his anger

simmer and boil over into his next five races, winning them all.

"I can almost pinpoint that race as the moment when Michael stepped up," NBAC coach Tom Himes said. "He didn't cry. He didn't throw his goggles. . . . It's like he said to himself, 'I'm going to get this guy next time.'"

Although Michael liked swimming the butterfly stroke best, he excelled in the other strokes too. Swimming events are divided: named by distances, given in meters or sometimes in feet, and by four

Breaststroke

Breaststroke is one of the four competitive strokes. It is the slowest stroke but perhaps the hardest to learn. It is also the easiest of the four to make a disqualifying error in, particularly for younger, inexperienced swimmers.

One of the reasons breaststroke is the slowest stroke is head position. In freestyle the swimmer can control when to rotate to breath. In breast the head is underwater for half the stroke and above the water for the other half. The legs remain underwater the entire time. The breaststroke kick involves both legs at the same time. It is usually described as a "frog" or "whip kick."

strokes — freestyle, butterfly, breast, and back. The length of an Olympic-sized pool is fifty meters, but in the United States swimmers also compete in twenty-five meter pools. Swimming is often divided into short course—twenty-five meter pools—in the winter and long course—fifty-meter pools—in the summer.

Most events center on one stroke, with the exception of the individual medley (IM) combining the four strokes. Teams of swimmers also compete in relay events, such as the 4x100 freestyle relay, in which four different swimmers each swim 100 meters freestyle. There are also medley relays, in which each of the four swimmers swims a different stroke.

Michael's skill occasionally caused him problems with his teammates. As he moved up through the ranks at NBAC, he started training with swimmers who were six or seven years older. They didn't like losing to "Little Phelps" and sometimes picked on him, tossing him back and forth over the pool lanes. They once stuffed him in a trash can and piled equipment on top of him. They also teased him about his big ears and his lisp, laughing when he tried to say the letter *s*.

At one meet, two swimmers threw Michael's soap and clothes around one of the boy's bathrooms. They

Michael's competitors would often tease him about his big ears and his lisp. *(Courtesy of AP Images)*

picked on Michael and shouted his name. Bob Bowman, NBAC's newest coach, charged into the bathroom, yelling at Michael. Even though Michael shouted back, denying any wrongdoing, the coach would not listen and scolded Michael. Bowman left the bathroom shaking his head and mumbling about Michael being uncoachable. The feeling of dislike was mutual.

"He'd [Bowman] seen me at the pool, running around and being benched, and said, 'There's no way I'm training him,'" said Michael.

Even so, Bowman was charged with coaching the group that ranged from eleven-year-old Michael to high school seniors. Many feared Bowman. A "Beware of Bob" sign hung on his door. To hide his anxiety Michael tried to drive his new coach crazy. But if Michael swam nine laps instead of ten, Bowman caught him. When

Bob Bowman *(Courtesy of Doug Benc/Getty Images)*

Michael arrived one minute late for a five o'clock practice, Bowman was waiting by the door to grill him about being late. If he splashed others, Bowman lectured him. When Michael hopped in and out of the water, hid people's caps and goggles, and chased a girl he liked with a cap full of water, Bowman told Michael he was supposed to be tired after practice; Michael retorted that he didn't get tired.

Michael and his new coach differed in many ways. Bowman analyzed the motions of swimming, while Michael gave little thought to improving the efficiency of his strokes. Bowman was an avid reader, while Michael had trouble in school. Bowman studied French, and Michael was versed in pop culture and ESPN. Bowman also came from a traditional southern home, while Michael came from a home divided by divorce.

Even though they clashed, Bowman began to see Michael differently after one particularly grueling practice. He'd assigned a set that included a 400 freestyle, a 400 IM, a 4x100 stroke, and a 4x100 freestyle, each repeated three times. Michael pushed through the set, despite the rigorous intensity. At the end he began to speed up, finishing faster than he'd been swimming at the beginning. Michael didn't realize what he was doing, but Bowman did.

Bowman began to alter all of Michael's strokes, reshaping and refining them to make them more efficient. Michael practiced a few laps with a new kicking style Bowman wanted, then out of rebellion and laziness switched back to his old habit. When he refused to accept Bowman's coaching, he got thrown out of practice. This happened every day for a week; Michael was furious and Bowman knew it.

He explained:

> The thing that got Michael the most, and still does, is to take swimming away from him. He hated to be excused early. He considered that an embarrassment. He knew practice was important; he was raised on that concept. Because of his ADHD, it was one thing that came naturally and felt good. It probably calmed him down. He always left practice in a better state than when he arrived.

But still Bowman challenged Michael. He suggested Michael wasn't mature enough to change. The next day Michael proved Bowman wrong. Although he chafed under Bowman's discipline, he also improved. Bowman sometimes had him practice using only one arm so Michael could concentrate on the way his arms moved through the water. He taught him to keep his elbows high during the freestyle, pulling through the water with his fingertips and letting his legs do the work. Sometimes Michael practiced the strokes using just his legs. To increase his resistance in the water and strengthen him, Bowman had Michael swim tethered to a pulley, or swim in a scuba vest or while wearing his sneakers.

Bowman realized Michael had a swimmer's body, with big hands that moved water. He had a massive arm span of six-feet and seven-inches. Michael's short legs kept him from dragging in the water, and his size

Michael has a swimmer's body with large hands and an expansive arm span. *(Courtesy of Victor Spinelli/WireImage)*

fourteen feet acted like flippers. Being double-jointed also gave him flexibility other swimmers didn't have. Michael moved awkwardly on land, but was made to swim.

A month after officials named Athens, Greece the location for the 2004 Olympic Games, Bowman met with Michael's parents. He shared his thoughts on Michael's talent, determination, and attitudes. Bowman saw Michael swimming faster in practice and at meets without tiring. He explained that Michael's talent would send him to the Olympics in 2004. If Michael continued to develop as he had, he might even be ready for the 2000 Olympics in Sydney, Australia.

If Michael took this chance the commitment would be all consuming, with the potential for crushing disappointment like his sister's. Michael would have to give up the other sports he played and dedicate his life to swimming: living in the water, eating, breathing, and sleeping for swimming. He would swim for five hours each day, seven days a week, without breaks for holidays. Michael's mother worried her son was too young for such pressure. But after weighing all of these factors, twelve-year-old Michael set his sights on Olympic glory.

two

The Land Down Under

As Michael began his path to the Olympics, he also started his first year at Dumbarton Middle School. Before and after school he dedicated his life to swimming, but at school he was a fish out of water. He wrote and passed notes to girls but struggled to keep a journal for English class. Although he devoured each month's copy of *Swimming World* magazine searching for his name, he disliked reading assignments.

As Bowman honed his skills in the water, his parents helped him on land. His mother taught him patience and attention to detail. When Michael decided to wean himself off of Ritalin, his mother supported him, and he learned how to set a difficult goal and succeed. After being suspended for punching someone who flicked his ears, Michael listened as his mother talked to him about resolving conflicts with words. In contrast, his father taught him better punching technique.

"Michael, if you're going to hit the kid," he said, "make it a good one."

Michael's father took him fishing and to baseball games. Sometimes he worked as an official at meets, offering Michael encouragement before and after his races. Michael also liked that his father worked at the starting block end.

"There wasn't much chance I'd get disqualified," Michael said, "even if I dove in a week early and threw fishnets in the other seven lanes."

Fred Phelps taught his son to look strangers in the eye and to shake hands firmly. But the two saw each other infrequently. Fred had begun to work with special weapons and tactics (SWAT) teams, although mostly he continued to inspect vehicles on highways. Debbie Phelps also had moved her family to a townhouse ten minutes from Meadowbrook. But Fred lived on the other side of Baltimore and couldn't always come to his son's meets.

When Bowman moved a street away from Michael's new house, some suggested he represented a father figure for Michael. There was no denying he was a major

influence in Michael's life. By the year 2003, they would have spent more than 2,000 days together.

Even so, despite the decision to shoot for the Olympics, Michael and his coach continued to fight. He still tried to get away with things behind Bowman's back. He and other swimmers invented a language they figured Bowman couldn't understand, until he wrote down their practice schedule using the language. Michael also tried to shorten some of Bowman's schedules by fooling around or swimming slowly. After one of these sessions Bowman hauled Michael out of the pool.

"Michael is not on the team unless he does the set I told him to do yesterday." Bowman said when he met with Michael's parents the next morning. Michael sat in his cap and pouted. "Michael, I don't care if you don't like it, and I really don't care if you like me, but if you want to be on this team, you have to get in the pool and finish what you were supposed to do yesterday." Realizing Bowman was serious, Michael went downstairs and completed the drill.

Bowman was tough on Michael because he saw his potential. They continued to train as Michael worked his way through middle school and started high school at Towson High in 1999. Despite their differences Michael and Bowman began to communicate wordlessly, each reading the other. Bowman could everywhere they can reach, friends help shave where they can't.

"Shaving a guy's back is a little like taking cough syrup," Michael said. "But it has to be done."

By 2000, Michael was ahead of his training schedule. He'd had a growth spurt, which boosted his confidence and increased the length of his strokes. At the end of March he and Bowman went to the USA Swimming Summer Nationals in Seattle, Washington. They ate every meal at a restaurant next to their hotel. For seven days straight, breakfast, lunch, and dinner Michael started his meal with clam chowder and ended with a slab of cheesecake. His teammates nicknamed him Mr. Clam Chowder and called it his secret weapon.

At the meet, Michael crushed the age group record for the 200 butterfly. He also broke a record in the 400 IM, dropping his own time by seven seconds, in a sport where hundredths of seconds make a difference. Bowman didn't reveal his excitement, not wanting to inflate Michael's hopes. But he realized Michael might qualify for the Olympics that year in Australia, four years ahead of schedule. Bowman sat down with Michael's mother and told her to prepare herself for the hype that would follow her son soon. They had Michael apply for a passport, telling him

he might need it someday, but not mentioning the Olympics.

In August, Michael headed to the U.S. Olympic Trials in Indianapolis, Indiana along with his mother,

Butterfly Stroke

The butterfly is perhaps the most difficult swimming stroke to master. Although it appears to depend almost totally on sheer strength, to master the "fly" a swimmer has to use several actions at the same time.

The butterfly uses a dolphin kick. In a dolphin kick the swimmer keeps the legs together, with the feet in a downward position, and uses an undulation motion to propel. The swimmer may make as many strokes and kicks as he or she likes. However, the goal in all swimming is to make as few strokes, kicks, and breaths as possible.

The butterfly stroke evolved from the breaststroke. Both strokes require the use of both arms at the same time, along with the dolphin kick. Butterfly times are usually better than breaststroke times because the swimmer remains underwater for longer periods.

father, and Whitney. Although he was one of the best swimmers in the country, Michael was only two months past his fifteenth birthday and had just gotten his braces removed. He stayed in his own hotel room

learned to drink only from taped-up coolers, meaning an official had poured in the water or sports drink. Doctors also tested him for Marfan's Syndrome, a condition affecting the body's connective tissue. It can be fatal if there is leakage in the blood vessels leading to the heart. Having long hands and feet, as well as an arm span that's longer than one's height, can be an early warning sign. The test results were normal, but Michael had to be checked yearly to ensure his safety.

He and fellow NBAC swimmer Jamie Barone also helped each other in one of a swimmer's least favorite jobs—shaving. Swimmers shave their body hair to reduce friction and drag in the water. They shave

Removing body hair increases a swimmer's lap time. *(Courtesy of AP Images)*

Towson High School *(Courtesy of James G. Howes)*

tilt his head or make a hand movement and Michael
would know what to do. During races, coaches
whistle to their swimmers; Michael could recognize
Bowman's pitch.

"There's the one that says 'Good job. Keep up the
same pace.' . . . And there's the half-whistle, half-
slap of the hands that says 'What the heck is up with
you today? Get that gorilla off your back and start
swimming,'" Michael said.

At age fourteen, Michael also began to see the
downside of swimming. As he entered more serious
competitions, he had to take drug tests, as some
athletes boost their performance with drugs. Michael

An aerial view of Sydney, Australia

The Thorpedo, Thorpe was the stuff of legend in his home country and Australian fans had hopes of his Olympic domination. The Thorpedo had been named the best swimmer in the world twice. At six-feet and four-inches tall, he had giant feet and wore size seventeen shoes. Michael had spent months studying a video of Thorpe, analyzing his strokes and dolphin-style kick while turning. Michael also noted Thorpe's smooth confidence out of the pool and his deft answers during interviews.

On August 20, 2000, Michael and Bowman flew to Pasadena, California, where they met other swimmers on the U.S. team en route to Australia. Michael's mother gave him a long checklist of items to pack. She and the rest of his family would follow him to

Ian Thorpe *(Courtesy of AP Images/David Guttenfelder)*

Sydney. Michael joined other teenagers on the U.S. team—Aaron Peirsol, Ian Crocker, Klete Keller, and Erik Vendt. As a surprise their flight attendant took the teens into the cockpit so they could overlook Sydney's harbor, graced by its modern white opera house.

Olympic athletes from around the world stay in the Olympic Village—dorm rooms, souvenir shops, restaurants, a post office, a theater, a laundromat, and a cafeteria. Michael roomed with teammate Aaron Peirsol. They talked about becoming the youngest Americans to win medals. Although Michael's coach

had daily pool deck passes, because he wasn't on the Olympic staff he had no access to the Village. Susan Teeter, the team's assistant manager, served as Bowman's eyes and ears. Michael's coach worried because older athletes sometimes threw wild parties when their events ended, and Michael was only fifteen years old. When Teeter phoned Bowman after Michael blew off curfew and goofed around in the hallway, Michael got a scolding over the phone.

The 2000 Olympics opened with a dazzling show of psychedelic colors and lights, then featured men on horseback and a tribute to Australia's Aborigines. Michael was a novice to the Olympics. While other swimmers rested for their events he attended Olympic

The Olympic village in Sydney, Australia *(Courtesy of Matt Turner/Allsport)*

baseball games. He also hung out in the video arcade after he fried the U.S. team's video game system by plugging it in without an electrical adapter.

His youth and inexperience almost lost him his first Olympic race in the 200 butterfly. In Sydney swimmers were announced before the race according to their times, unlike in the U.S. where swimmers were called by their lane number. In lane four, Michael was one of the last to be announced, but didn't realize it. He wasn't ready when the race began. Although he dove in with everyone else, he did not have time to tie the strings on his swimsuit. The suit stayed on, but the strings flapped for the entire race. Despite the rocky start Michael advanced from the preliminaries to the semifinals.

Michael and his coach joked about his swimsuit mishap, but when the same thing happened again that night in the semifinal, Bowman chewed him out for not being better prepared. Michael squeaked into third place, qualifying him for the final the next day.

On September 19, as Michael prepared to board the shuttle bus to get to his final, he realized he'd accidentally grabbed his roommate's photo identification. Athletes need their official credentials to get them through security checkpoints and into competition sites. Michael panicked and ran back to his room, where he found his identification. The trip cost him thirty minutes of warm-up time, adding to his frazzled nerves.

Michael finished fifth in the race, with a time that would have won every previous Olympic final. He missed medaling by four-tenths of a second. Although disappointed, he watched the world's best swimmers, such as gold medalists Ian Thorpe from Australia and Pieter van den Hoogenband from the Netherlands. Michael tucked away these experiences.

The following day Michael met with his mother, father, uncle, aunts, and his father's partner, Jackie. Away from the rest of the group Fred told Michael that he and Jackie had married a month before. Michael was stunned and hurt that his father hadn't told him earlier. Fred said he didn't want to distract Michael from focusing on the Olympics, but the news caused the rift between the two to widen.

Michael and Bowman left Sydney before the closing ceremonies of the Olympics. His mother arranged for a limousine full of his friends to meet Michael at the Baltimore airport. In celebration, they went to a convenience store for Slurpees. He returned to Towson High School one month late for his sophomore year. On Sunday, September 30, he slept late for the first time in months. As Michael slept, the Sydney

Fireworks over the Sydney Harbour Bridge during closing ceremonies of the Olympic games in Sydney, Australia

Olympics came to a close on the other side of the world as fireworks lit up the Australian night sky.

Michael's hometown and school gave their returning Olympian a hero's welcome. He threw out the first pitch at a Baltimore Orioles game, received a team jersey from players on the Baltimore Ravens, and traveled to the White House with the Olympic team for a picture with President Bill Clinton. Michael also got a tattoo of the Olympic rings on his hip, following a tradition among Olympic swimmers.

While being an Olympian had its perks, it also made Michael miss having fun with his friends. He couldn't participate in many activities, such as sled riding, because he might injure himself. He had to take care when playing basketball, his friends calling *watch out* and *behind you*, as they joked that none of them wanted to be the one responsible for ruining Michael's swimming career. He grew angry with the grind of training; Bowman's pushing and yelling infuriated him. After the two had a screaming match, Michael considered quitting the sport. In the end, he reconsidered and Bowman became more supportive.

Michael runs onto the playing field as an honorary guest of the Baltimore Ravens. *(Courtesy of Doug Pensinger/Getty Images)*

Michael had lost a father figure when Fred remarried. Now Bowman taught him how to drive and arranged for him to mentor a young swimmer with cancer, which gave Michael a new perspective on courage and determination. He trod a fine line between world-famous swimmer and teenager.

In 2001, Michael traveled to the Spring Nationals in Texas. At the competition in the 200 butterfly he set his first world record. Four months shy of turning sixteen, Michael was the youngest man ever to set a world record.

"Nobody has ever done that race faster than you," Michael said to himself. "That's awesome."

He called his mother, so excited he could hardly tell her he'd broken a world record. "I just started giggling, like a kid in a candy store who is embarrassed by how good he feels," Michael said. He didn't hear from his father. When Michael returned to Baltimore, his mother and sister Hilary tried to celebrate by taking him out to a restaurant in Baltimore's Inner Harbor. When they discovered there was nearly a three-hour wait, Hilary joked he should tell them about his world record.

After the Spring Nationals, a Japanese film crew visited Meadowbrook to talk to Michael about the upcoming World Championships in Fukuoka, Japan.

Before traveling to the event the swim staff briefed the swimmers on Japanese etiquette: they shouldn't tip waiters, as it wasn't common practice, they might be asked to take off their shoes and put on slippers before entering a room, and they shouldn't eat street food, avoiding the possibility of food poisoning.

In Fukuoka, Michael set a blistering pace in the 200 butterfly, breaking his own world record and winning his first world title. At the end of the race Michael squinted through his goggles, unsure he'd read his time on the scoreboard correctly. He celebrated by ordering a corn dog, French fry, and lasagna feast in his hotel room that night.

Michael took away two memories from Japan. The Fukuoka Grand Hyatt hotel had impressed him: it had a computer station in the main room, two huge beds, a television in the bathroom, and a seat warmer on the toilet. He and roommate Jamie Raush, a breaststroker on the U.S. team, had awakened each other in the mornings by whacking each other with pillows.

Michael's other memory was of Ian Thorpe, who won the 200, 400, and 800 freestyles and anchored the Australian team in three relays. Michael set his sights on beating The Thorpedo at their next meeting.

During his junior year, sixteen-year-old Michael signed a contract with the swimsuit company Speedo. The new contract paid him nearly $100,000 annually, with a clause to pay for his college education if his swimming career didn't pan out. Soon he was working at Speedo swimming clinics and attending photo shoots. At first Michael had difficulties, accidentally wearing Nike brand shoes to a Speedo photo shoot, and making clumsy attempts to work in his sponsor's name during interviews.

Michael gave more interviews, although answering questions didn't come naturally. He tended to rely on one word throughout the entire interview, such as when he said, "It was an unbelievably unbelievable meet, if you can believe it." He also learned to say *No comment* to questions about his love life.

"You always give the same answers," one reporter said.

"They always ask the same questions," Michael responded.

Reporters analyzed and quoted Michael's answers, and fans posted them on the Internet. He had little privacy, as did his coach, family, and friends.

Still Michael enjoyed other benefits of turning pro. He furnished his bedroom with a forty-six inch high-definition television, bought a Cadillac Escalade for himself, and gave his mother a Mercedes Benz for

Christmas. He also talked about getting a dog, after seeing two English bulldogs in a pet store window. He wanted to name them Diesel and Chief, but he had little time for a dog. Michael's life consisted of waking, eating, training, and resting.

Each of Michael's workouts involved swimming a certain distance, such as 100 meters, with a varied number of repetitions. When he worked on building speed Michael logged 60,000 meters a week, nearly 800 of which he swam at his race pace. Other times he swam for endurance, logging 80,000 meters each week, like completing a marathon each day. Michael practiced 550 times a year, not taking a day off for five years straight—even training the day of his prom. By the 2004 Olympics, Michael had completed enough miles to swim from the Chesapeake Bay to the Aegean Sea and back again. The Olympics to be held in Athens, Greece were approaching.

three

The Human Shark

In some ways Michael Phelps was a typical seventeen-year-old. He had little interest in his schoolwork, loved rap music, and tried to impress girls with his cool new car. To keep from being teased about his big ears, he wore a baseball cap tugged down low over his unruly dark hair. Phelps was fiercely protective of his single mother.

He also ate constantly, like many teenagers. But Phelps took even normal teenage eating habits to an extreme. He and Jamie Barone frequented Pete's Grille, a diner in Baltimore. Phelps's usual at Pete's consisted of three fried egg sandwiches topped with cheese, lettuce, tomatoes, fried onions, and mayonnaise, then an omelet, a bowl of grits, three slices of French toast, and three chocolate chip pancakes followed by a milkshake. Along with Phelps's friend Matt Townsend they had eating contests at all-you-can-eat buffets and chicken wing joints, where Phelps won one dollar for downing fifty wings. Another time his ability to hold his breath, after years of swimming, came in handy when the three placed bets about swallowing a goldfish.

Phelps took other events to extremes as well. At the 2002 Summer Nationals in Florida he set a world record in the 400 IM. Next he and Bowman traveled to Japan for the Pan Pacific competition, which included swimmers from the United States, Australia, Canada, Japan, China, and other Pacific Rim nations.

In Japan swimming is wildly popular. Japanese fans called Phelps "The Human Shark." They mobbed him for autographs and made crank calls to his hotel room. A female fan repeatedly tried to get into his room. Phelps began to use the alias Robert Davisson; Robert after Bowman's first name and Davisson after his mother's maiden name.

Phelps left Japan with three gold and two silver medals. He helped the U.S. team lower the world record in the 4x100 relay. During the 800 freestyle relay Phelps had given the Americans a lead over the Australians for the first time in six years. Although Thorpe restored order and anchored his team to victory in the race they owned, Phelps had gotten Thorpe's attention.

One night on the long bus ride back to the hotel Phelps and Thorpe talked about training, celebrity, and the possibility of one day working out together in Sydney or Baltimore. Despite their conversation their rivalry remained strong.

Phelps continued his streak in Thorpe's homeland at The Duel in the Pool competition. In the 400 IM, Phelps lowered his own world-record pace by six seconds. Just forty minutes later he missed breaking another world record on the 100 butterfly by the length of a fingernail. Within two hours Phelps claimed a third win in the 200 butterfly. The Australian Olympic champion Grant Hackett advised Phelps against spreading himself so thin. Oblivious, Phelps was busy trying to decide how to spend his $25,000 bonus he got from USA Swimming for breaking his own world record.

After the competition Phelps met his parents in the hotel ballroom. While he and his father talked, Phelps turned to acknowledge a fan. Annoyed, his father walked away. The gulf between father and son widened further, but Phelps was actually learning from his father. Years before, Fred berated a baseball player for ignoring Michael's polite autograph request.

Now the tables were turned and Phelps was giving the autographs. His agent tried to get him to take less time by signing his initials and dragging the pen.

"You want to give a kid that?" Phelps said. "You can't even read it. If he shows it to his friends, they won't think, 'Oh, cool, Michael Phelps;' they'll think 'Yeah, right—Mi___P___.'" He continued to take his time.

In June of 2003, he graduated from Towson High. His friends headed to Ocean City, Maryland, for a week of celebration. But Phelps, and nine other elite swimmers, traveled to Greece, where the 2004 Olympics would begin in 382 days. The swimmers toured the aquatic center and Olympic Village. They viewed the Acropolis, a flat-topped rock towering above

The Parthenon in Athens, Greece

Athens. Perched atop the Acropolis stood the stark white columns and ruins of The Parthenon, a temple built more than 2,000 years before as a tribute to the goddess Athena. The swimmers also strolled through the mazelike streets of the *Plaka*, an old neighborhood filled with colorful cafes, museums, and shops beneath the Acropolis. They experienced the heat and humidity that would sap their energy. At the end of July they headed home. Before the Olympics began, there were many more races to tackle.

At a competition in California, in an outdoor pool choppy from the wind, Phelps lowered the world record for the 200 IM. He was the first male swimmer in thirty-six years to set a world record without shaving his body hair. On his last day as a seventeen-year-old, Phelps had broken the oldest swimming record on the books. He'd also started the race from a dead stop after slipping on a puddle of water on his starting block and falling, instead of diving into the water. Phelps now held world records in three events.

The World Championships in Barcelona, Spain, just three weeks away, were considered a testing ground for the Olympics. If Phelps continued his impressive streak he could become the front-runner for the Olympics. Others wanted that role, and competitive trash talking began.

"We've got Ian Thorpe, and they're trying to say they've got someone even better," said Australian coach Don Talbot, when he heard of Phelps's latest record. "In the major international meets, Phelps has done nothing yet. We know Phelps is a good boy, but people trying to say he's a greater swimmer than Ian—that's absolute nonsense . . . for people saying he's going to outdo Thorpie, I live to see that day."

Bowman printed out the article and showed it to Phelps. In Barcelona Phelps would need to draw from that motivation and rely on his rituals to calm his nerves at the pressure-packed competition. Before racing, he listened to rap music on his iPod, creating his own world and keeping these songs in his head as he swam. His especially liked songs by Eminem, Biggie, and G-Unit. One of his favorites was "Party Up" by DMX, which he had listened to before breaking his first world record. Over and over he also listened to the lyrics of Eminem's song "Till I Collapse."

> Sometimes you feel tired, feel weak
> When you feel weak, you feel like you wanna just
> give up
> But you gotta search within you, find that inner
> strength

Phelps had other rituals too. Before each race he bent down, reaching his arms above his head. Then he

Michael crosses his arms across his chest during his pre-race warm-up ritual. *(Courtesy of AP Images/Mark J. Terrill)*

swung his arms back down three times, fast across his chest. After the mishap in California he added another step to his ritual—toweling off the starting block.

Confident in his abilities, Phelps asked his mother if he could get a dog for breaking a world record in Spain. He had received two passes to the competition which he'd given to his mother and sister Hilary. Phelps's father thought one of the passes should have been his and didn't attend the event. Phelps retorted that his mother and sister had attended his competitions for years while his father wasn't around.

On the first day of the World Championships, Phelps opened by lowering his own world record in the semifinals of the 200 butterfly. In the stands his sister Hilary held up a handmade sign that said "Dog?" The following day Phelps won the finals in the 200 butterfly, set an American record in the 200 freestyle, and led the U.S. relay team to second place in the 800 freestyle relay. That evening people applauded when he entered the dining room of the Hotel Fira Palace, where the U.S. team was staying.

Next Phelps set another world record in the semifinals of the 200 IM. Hilary held up a sign—"2 Dogs?"

During the competition a woman in a green suit approached Debbie Phelps.

"What's this about a rivalry between our boys?" she asked. The woman was Margaret Thorpe, Ian's mother. Both women were schoolteachers and also had daughters who excelled in swimming. They talked about experiences that few mothers around the world could relate to, devoting their lives to swimming and watching their sons swim faster than anyone in history.

The following day Phelps took his regular afternoon nap, which fit in well with the Spanish siesta when shops closed for the afternoon. Then in the evening he lowered the world record in the

semifinals of the 100 butterfly; this time Hilary's sign read—"3 Dogs?" Phelps had little time to celebrate as he faced a field of fresh swimmers in the finals of the 200 IM. But he jumped in the pool, lowered another world record, and bested his rival Ian Thorpe, who finished second. His sister held up another sign—"4 Dogs?" Phelps joined the only two men in history who held world records simultaneously in four events—American swimming legend Mark Spitz and German swimmer Michael Gross, dubbed *Albatross* because of his 6'11" arm span.

After the race Phelps headed for a press conference with Thorpe and Italy's Massi Rossalino, the bronze

Mark Spitz

The first athlete to win seven gold metals, Mark Spitz became one of the few positive stories to come out of the 1972 Munich Olympics.

Spitz when into the Olympics that summer after being built up as the world's greatest swimmer. Instead of letting the pressure get to him, he rose to the occasion and not only won the gold but also set new world records in each of the events.

Spitz won his glory in the most tragic Olympiad ever. At 4:30 in the morning of September 5, Palestinian terrorists committed to destroying the state of Israel broke into the compound where the athletes were staying. They killed two Israelis and took nine hostages. Spitz, who is Jewish, spoke out against the terrorist action the next morning before leaving. The nine hostages were later murdered.

After the Olympics Spitz garnered several lucrative endorsement deals and attempted to launch a career in entertainment. Although he was not successful in his new endeavor, he remained the most famous American swimmer ever until Michael Phelps arrived on the scene.

Spitz eventually began working in real estate and lives in Los Angles with his family.

medalist. A reporter asked Phelps what music he listened to before the race, which was Eminem. The next reporter asked Rossalino what he would do to beat Phelps next time.

"The first thing I'm going to do is buy that CD," Rossalino said. "Then I will listen to all the songs and see if one of them can make me swim that fast."

Phelps's performance caused a buzz. Newspapers in Spain dubbed him *El Nuevo Spitz*, or "the New Mark Spitz." Twenty-four hours later these comparisons stopped. On his morning off Phelps tried to meet his mother for lunch, but she was Christmas shopping. Disappointed he turned his attention to the finals of

the 100 butterfly later that day, confident he'd win. Before the race his iPod malfunctioned, throwing off his concentration. Then in a stunning upset American swimmer Ian Crocker flashed past Phelps in the final, breaking his world record. Upset, Phelps sat by the pool in disbelief.

"You need to think about which Michael Phelps they'll see at the press conference," Bowman counseled him quietly. "Are you going to pout or be a champion?

Newspapers ran the story with the headline "*Phelps es Humano,*" or "Phelps is Human." Bowman blamed himself for letting Phelps get too loose. He'd watched him signing autographs, joking with the Australians, and talking to friends on the deck.

"I had been walking on air all week," Bowman said. "It's healthy to come back to the reality of the situation. It's not a fairy tale . . . Getting beat is tough for someone who seldom gets beat."

On the final day of the competition Phelps won the 400 IM and set another world record. His sister held up one final sign—"5 Dogs? At the competition in Spain men and women from 150 countries set nine world records; Phelps set five of them. But after his disappointing finish in the 100 butterfly he became more receptive to Bowman's prodding and cursing.

Phelps found little time to relax in the days following

the world championships. Distance and training demands caused him and his girlfriend of six months to break up. After the World Championships, Phelps would face even more demanding competitions. The relationship was one more thing Phelps was forced to give up in his quest to become the fastest swimmer on the planet.

Ten days later Phelps swam at the Summer Nationals in College Park, Maryland, just an hour's drive from his home. He collected five more titles, winning the 200 backstroke, the 100 freestyle, the 200 and 400 freestyles, and the 200 IM. His last event had been the 200 IM. Bowman promised to shave his head if Phelps broke one of the world records he'd set in Spain. In the race Phelps lowered his world record, forcing Bowman to make good on his bet. It was Phelps's seventh world record in forty-one days.

On the heels of his success, Phelps renegotiated his contract with Speedo. His compensation would be nearly $400,000 a year. The swimwear company also promised Phelps a one million dollar bonus after the 2004 or 2008 Olympics if he matched Mark Spitz's 1972 Olympic record of seven gold medals. The news was huge for a sport that received little recognition apart from Olympic years, but this

Michael appears at an event to promote Speedo, one of his sponsors. *(Courtesy of Paul Andrew Hawthorne/WireImage)*

amount paled in comparison to similarly aged athletes in baseball and basketball.

After the intense competition Phelps took a brief 109-day break before heading to a pair of meets in two Australian cities, where Ian Thorpe reigned. Swimming is one of the most popular sports in Australia. Australians listed Thorpe as their most wanted Christmas guest, followed by actress Nicole Kidman and actor Russell Crowe. Ninety percent of Australians live within six miles of the ocean. Appreciative of his talent at their favorite sport, Australians gave Phelps a warm welcome when he arrived for competitions in Sydney and Melbourne.

The meet in Sydney was well produced. Spectators paid admission fees and received glossy programs. The televised races showcased athletes from several continents. Phelps had a driver, a custom-tailored tuxedo hanging in his hotel room closet, and knowledgeable fans in the stands. While Thorpe whipped a tired Phelps in one event, Phelps won his two other races. On Thanksgiving Day Phelps headed to Melbourne where he won all six of his events at the meet. Besides earning $20,000 he won five blenders and a mixer—one of the meet's sponsors manufactured kitchen appliances and provided prizes.

Bowman kept Phelps mentally sharp during the meet, arranging details so Phelps would stay on his toes. He asked their driver to pick up Phelps late so he had to spend more time waiting at the pool. He also made sure a few of the meals Phelps ordered weren't right. Bowman wanted Phelps to learn to deal with small stresses and not have it throw him off during more important events. Bowman couldn't

plan for all the stressful events. At one point some wild fans started following Phelps. A swimmer from Germany helped by switching cars and exchanging caps with Phelps. The fans followed the German swimmer's car while Phelps escaped.

Phelps and his coach found themselves arguing more as the stakes grew higher and the Olympics neared. When Phelps returned from a twenty-five day road trip, filled with different hotels and airports, Bowman still drove him hard. Exhausted and jet lagged, Phelps informed Bowman he needed time off and stomped out of the pool.

As Athens drew nearer, sponsors flocked to Phelps. He signed deals with Argent Mortgage, AT&T Wireless, Visa, and Omega Watchmakers. Visa gave most Americans their first glimpse of Michael Phelps with a commercial called "Lap." The spot showed Phelps swimming past ancient Greek ruins and a fishing boat in the Aegean Sea. After swimming through towering waves in the Atlantic Ocean, there was a close up of Phelps touching the base of the Statue of Liberty in New York Harbor. He said, "One," and turned around to swim back for another lap.

Prior to events in Athens, Phelps faced the Olympic Trials in California. A week before the Trials, he and his family quietly celebrated his nineteenth birthday. Phelps also invited his father to dinner as their relationship was improving. With Phelps focused on the Olympics he had little time to repair the relationship, but his father tried to fit into his son's life in little ways. They had lunch at Pete's Grille, e-mailed, text messaged, and watched football together.

As the family dined on sushi, one of Phelps's favorite foods, they savored their family time. Phelps faced the Trials in July and the Olympics in August. He had planned a nationwide tour for September and to start attending the University of Michigan in Ann Arbor in October. This wouldn't be the last time they celebrated birthdays together, but it might be the last time they all called Baltimore home.

For months Phelps had kept a calendar on his bedroom wall, checking off the days to the Trials. He would be competing in six events, four of which he'd set records in at the World Championships. But concerns beyond the races plagued him and his coach. When an unknown limousine service called to confirm details about transporting Phelps from the airport to the hotel, a quick phone call uncovered that the driver wasn't from a legitimate service. A search revealed that the driver's house was filled with Michael Phelps memorabilia. Sometimes fans

stole his possessions, kickboards, and water bottles as souvenirs. Sean Foley, a former swimmer from Texas, began to act as Phelps's bodyguard.

Nearly seven hundred entrants would compete at the Olympic Trials. Fewer than fifty of them would make it. The strain was overwhelming. Nerves about performance combined with fears of slipping on the starting block and false starting.

The Trials began on Wednesday, July 7, with a breeze from the Pacific Ocean cooling the air. Phelps hoped that his pace in the 400 IM would not only take him to the Olympics but break his record. After setting the record in Australia, Phelps had visited the Aquatic Center where the Olympic Trials would be held. In the parking lot he'd chalked his world record time, hoping to beat it. Now in Phelps's first final at the Trials he won the 400 IM, and broke his own world record. He became the first athlete to make the U.S. Olympic swim team.

On Friday, Phelps won the 200 freestyle, qualifying for his second Olympic event. Just forty-four minutes later he advanced to the finals of the 200 butterfly.

The next day Phelps's father unexpectedly hopped a cross-country flight, despite trying to save money for traveling to Athens. He watched his son win the

Mark Spitz raises Michael's arm during the awards ceremony of the 2004 Olympic Trials *(Courtesy of AP Images/Mark J. Terrill)*

200 butterfly, and qualify for his third Olympic event. That night Mark Spitz presented the awards and hung the gold medal around Phelps's neck.

"I'll be over in Athens to watch you, and I'm behind you all the way," he said. "I know what you're going through. I went through it once before . . . Go get 'em."

In front of the crowd of nearly 10,000 cheering fans, Spitz raised Phelps's arm like a boxing referee signaling a winner in a fight. Phelps got goose bumps as the crowd acknowledged that the swimming torch had been passed.

On Monday Phelps faced a taxing evening with two finals and a semifinal. He finished first in the finals of the 200 backstroke, and then twenty-five minutes later won the 200 IM, qualifying him for his fourth and fifth Olympic events. He also advanced to the

Backstroke

In the backstroke, the arm makes an almost full rotation in and out of the water. As the name indicates, it is swum on the back. In competition, the backstroke is the only event that begins in the water. The swimmer begins by propelling backward at the gun. Because it starts in the water the backstroke is the first leg of medley relays.

The leg movement is also similar to the "flutter kick" used in freestyle. However, the "dolphin" kick is allowed for use after starts and turns for a limited distance. The kick provides less propulsion than the "dolphin" or "whip kick" used in the butterfly and breaststrokes. There is also a body rotation, again similar to the frontal crawl, that reduces drag.

finals of the 100 butterfly. The next day Phelps raced for the seventeenth and final time in seven days. He won the 100 butterfly, making him eligible to swim six individual events at the Olympics.

During the Trials, Bowman monitored Phelps's lactate levels, taking blood samples from his ear lobe. The readings indicate a swimmer's oxygen debt: the harder the athlete works the more lactate he or she produces. Because of his enhanced lung capacity from years of swimming, Phelps produced half the lactate of his competitors. But he and Bowman decided to drop the 200 backstroke from Phelps's Olympic events. Although Phelps liked to peek at the scoreboard during the race, it was the one in which he produced the most lactate.

Phelps's fame spread. He gave interviews and appeared on the *Tonight Show* with host Jay Leno. Outside his hotel Phelps signed autographs, but Bowman recognized the fake limousine driver from California in the crowd. Phelps and his coach ordered their car to leave immediately. The crazed fan hopped into the passenger seat of a waiting car which ran several lights in pursuit. The hotel stationed guards in the parking garage to protect Phelps, but the fan had gotten too close for the second time in ten days.

Phelps couldn't focus on the worrisome aspects of his fame. He turned his attention to Athens. He'd been focused on the name of the ancient city for years. He had moments when he whispered the letters *A-T-H-E-N-S* to himself. Soon he would find himself competing next to the ancient ruins that marked the world's first Olympic Games.

four
The Ancient Games

In 2004 the Olympic Games returned to Greece, where they had begun 4,000 years before as a tribute to the Greek gods who were said to live on Mt. Olympus. What was first a 200-meter footrace has evolved into today's Olympic Games featuring over 10,000 athletes from two hundred countries around the world.

For the 2004 games, Olympic officials in Greece blended the ancient and the modern. Some events, such as the shot put, would be held a half-day's drive outside of Athens, in Olympia, the remote site of the original Olympics. Runners would race at Panathinaiko Stadium, where the Olympics were revived in 1896. The oval track lay at the base of the Acropolis.

In 2004, there was concern about the security measures in place to ensure the safety of the athletes. World events in the past had disrupted the games and threatened to do so again. In the 1940s World War II had stopped the Summer Olympics. In other years countries chose to boycott the games, refusing to send their athletes out of political principles. At times athletes from certain nations were banned from participating because of their country's practices. Officials wanted to avoid an event like the one that occurred at the 1972 Olympics in Munich, Germany when nine athletes from Israel were taken hostage and killed.

Fears of terrorism from Islamic extremists rocked the scheduled Olympics in 2004. Memories of

Rescue workers stand at the scene of a 2004 terrorist bombing in Madrid, Spain. Fears of terrorism plagued the 2004 Olympic games, causing some athletes to withdraw from the competition. *(Courtesy of AP Photo/ Peter Dejong)*

the coordinated terrorist attacks in New York and Washington DC on September 11, 2001 were still fresh. In March of 2004, 190 people had been killed in a series of bombings in Madrid, Spain. To exacerbate fears, Greece was ringed by unrest. There was tension between Greece and Turkey, and Greece's Balkan borders to the north were with Kosovo and Bosnia, the scene of bloody war during the 1990s.

"Think about it," swimmer Lenny Krayzelburg said. "For terrorists to make a statement there isn't a much bigger place than the Olympic Games."

American tourists avoided the Olympic Games. Journalists received gas masks, crash first-aid courses, and antiterrorism training before boarding flights to Greece. Half of the U.S. public believed that a terrorist attack on American athletes was likely. Some U.S. athletes, such as tennis player Serena Williams, withdrew from Olympic teams. Regardless, the United States was ready to send their best athletes to compete in the games.

Spectators around the world also heard rumors that the Olympic preparations in Athens were behind schedule. Neither the resurfacing of the marathon route nor the building of a retractable steel and glass roof over the Olympic stadium was finished. Questions especially arose concerning the Olympic

Aquatic Center. Finals in the swimming events would be held at night with a cooling evening breeze, but preliminary races would take place under the blazing hot Mediterranean sun. While competing against world-class swimmers, athletes would have to contend with the blinding glare of the sun and heat that would bake the concrete and synthetic surfaces until they were hot enough to burn skin. Officials pushed for an indoor facility, then settled for a canopy to cover the outdoor pools and shade the swimmers; now the canopy was in doubt as well and tempers flared.

"If they manage to get water in the pool, we'll be happy," said Elena Vaitsekhovskaia, a member of the press.

Phelps was ready, whether the pool was or not.

"A pool is a pool," he said. "Roof or no roof, I'm going to be there and hopefully ready to swim. I've swum outdoors before."

At the Olympics in Sydney four years earlier Phelps had been an anonymous and awkward fifteen-year-old who forgot to tie his swimsuit and carried his roommate's ID badge. Now journalists compared him to the Greek god Poseidon who ruled over the seas. He was posing with supermodels and answering reporters' questions about his opinions on politics. He had sponsors, his own Web site, and devoted fans. Phelps appeared in *Sports Illustrated* and *Time* magazine, and was featured on the front cover of the *Complete Book of the Summer Olympics,* along with American runner Marion Jones.

Phelps planned to swim in five individual events and hoped to swim on relay teams in three other events. He could potentially win eight gold medals, breaking Mark Spitz's record of seven gold medals won in a single Olympics.

Some suggested Phelps was attempting too many events. Ian Thorpe, who had won three gold and two silver medals in the 2000 Olympics, predicted Phelps would be disappointed. Others joked that if there were a doggy paddle event Phelps would have entered that too. At nineteen, Phelps was trying to do what no athlete had ever done.

On August 1 he took off from San Francisco for his overnight flight to Greece. The plane held the entire U.S. Olympic swim team of twenty-one men, twenty-two women, eight coaches, three managers, and Bowman, serving as an assistant coach. Before his trip Phelps stored snapshots of his car and his cat, named Sydney in honor of his first Olympics, on his cell phone. He programmed in the phone number of Pete's Grille to call his friends back in Baltimore and loaded his iPod full of rap songs.

Instead of anxiously waiting in the Olympic Village for the games to begin, the team stayed on Mallorca, an island off the coast of Barcelona, Spain. Rimmed by the blue Mediterranean Sea, the island's green pine forests, rocky cliffs, crystal beaches, and soft fine sand surrounded the athletes. Each swimmer passed the time differently. Teammate Gary Hall Jr. sunned himself as Phelps spent his mornings in the pool practicing his starts and turns. With his height and length he had difficultly tucking himself into a tight ball for his turns. Phelps also worked on keeping his body straight instead of bending at the waist as he dove off the starting block. These details could slow him in a race where fractions of a second would make the difference between a win and a loss. In between his workouts Phelps relaxed and played poker with his teammates.

The opening ceremony of the 2004 Olympic Games depicted Greek history and myth. Phelps watched television coverage of the event from his dorm in the Olympic Village, where he roomed with Lenny Krayzelburg. That night he also watched the movie *Miracle,* the story of the underdog U.S. Olympic hockey team that defeated the Soviet Union in 1980. At 10:00 pm he turned off the movie and tried to sleep. Some people were offended that Phelps didn't attend the ceremony, but they didn't know his grueling schedule. Olympic swimming stretched over eight days, and Phelps would swim seven of them, racing eighteen times counting preliminaries and finals. The temperatures would reach one hundred degrees Fahrenheit in the shade by midmorning, so hot that when one spectator took off his glasses and put them on a minute later he burned his forehead.

Phelps's Olympics began on Saturday morning, August 14. Wearing black jammers, a swimsuit from his hips to his knees, he advanced to the finals of the 400 IM. After his cool down, he took a shuttle back to the Olympic Village where he wolfed down pizza and pasta and tried to nap. That evening, at 7:30 pm, Phelps competed in the finals. During the race he kept a close eye on the competition. After realizing he would win he smiled through the water for the last twenty-five meters.

With a world record time, he became the first American to win a gold medal at the 2004 Olympic Games. Phelps's teammate Erik Vendt took the silver medal and the two dove over three lane markers to embrace. Phelps turned to the grandstand and found his mother.

At the awards ceremony, officials draped the medal over his shoulders and placed an olive wreath on his

Phelps became the first American to win a gold medal at the 2004 Olympic Games by winning the 400 IM with a world record time. *(Courtesy of AP Images/Mark J. Terrill)*

head. Phelps held his hand over his heart as "The Star Spangled Banner" played. Afterwards he met his mother and sister Hilary alongside the practice pool. Through the metal fence he held up his gold medal. Debbie Phelps reached through the fence to touch her son, and he placed the medal into her hands.

"Mom," he said. "Look what I did."

His mother cried, remembering when he brought her his first age-group award as a little boy.

The following morning Phelps qualified to swim in the finals of both the 200 freestyle and the 400 freestyle relay. A rookie on the relay team, Phelps would swim with teammates Neil Walker, Ian Crocker, and Jason Lezak. Even though Crocker was suffering from a cold, the team won a bronze medal in the event. Phelps now couldn't beat Spitz's record of seven gold medals. To match it he would need to sweep his next six events.

On Monday, August 16 after two preliminary rounds Phelps qualified to swim in the final of the 200 butterfly. He also faced the final of the 200 freestyle, where he would swim against Ian Thorpe and Pieter van den Hoogenband, the best freestylers in the world. Some said Phelps had little chance of winning and should skip the race. He didn't. Thorpe took gold, van den Hoogenband took silver, and Phelps won a bronze medal, with his personal best time for the race.

After three events Phelps had won one gold and two bronze medals. He was happy, but his chance to match Spitz's record had ended. In the stands a reporter approached Debbie Phelps.

"The world has left your son tonight," the reporter said.

"Excuse me?" she said.

"Well, now that he won't be able to match Spitz's record, there won't be as many people around him . . . the hype is over."

"Well, the swimming isn't over," Debbie retorted. "Michael isn't even halfway through his platform. He has a lot to show the world."

The following day Phelps competed in the final of the 200 butterfly. He won another gold medal, but later that day, he would face his greatest challenge, the 800 freestyle relay. He and teammates Ryan Lochte,

Peter Vanderkaay, and Klete Keller were about to race against the seemingly invincible Australian team, headed up by Ian Thorpe. The Australians hadn't been defeated in the event since 1998.

That night an evening breeze fanned the spectators of the relay final. A half mile into the race, only thirteen hundredths of a second separated the two teams. Then Phelps and his teammates captured the gold medal in one of the closest finishes in the Olympics. Phelps raised his hands up and screamed with the rest of his teammates. He had won his third gold medal. With tears in his eyes Phelps called it the best night of his life. He had defeated his rival, giving Thorpe his first loss in that race at an international competition.

Michael (center) celebrates with Peter Vanderkaay (left) and Ryan Lochte after winning a gold medal in the 800 freestyle relay. *(Courtesy of AP Photo/ Mark Baker)*

"We owned that race," said Australian swimmer Michael Klim. "They stole our race."

After the race Phelps's sister Hilary tossed him a stuffed animal, a bulldog, a tradition they'd started at the World Championships when her brother had asked for a dog. Now his parents, sisters, and relatives surrounded him in Athens during his success. His friends and family back in Baltimore watched as well. Phelps's grandmother, eighty-five-year-old Leoma Davisson, sat glued to her television. Although plenty of people would have watched as her grandson swam at the Olympics, she refused company.

"I like to watch Michael by myself, I can scream and cry and nobody sees me," she said. "Michael doesn't let anybody win."

Phelps had seven races left for the games. He hoped for an eighth, by winning a spot on the 4x100 U.S. medley relay team.

The next day Phelps qualified for the final of the 200 IM. He sipped Carnation Instant Breakfast drink on the way to the practice pool, but vowed to find a McDonalds when his racing was done. Reporters wrote about Phelps drinking milk, which doctors called the ultimate power drink, during the Olympics. It contrasted starkly with the doping scandals in which some Olympic athletes were disqualified for their

use of performance-enhancing drugs. Like the other athletes Phelps was subject to random drug testing during the games. Each night he gave Bowman his medals to hold while officials tested him. Sometimes Bowman, so focused on the next race, forgot he had the medals in his pocket and accidentally set off metal detectors around the sites.

On Thursday Phelps buried his competition during the 200 IM final, taking the gold medal. After the medal ceremony he tossed his olive wreath to his mother and once again turned his attention back to the pool. Just thirty-one minutes later both he and Ian Crocker passed through to the semifinals of the 100 butterfly. The fastest American in the 100 butterfly would claim the spot to swim the butterfly for the U.S. relay team in the 4x100 medley relay.

American swimmer Gary Hall Jr. argued against Phelps racing on the team, claiming his lack of experience slowed the team in the first relay. Phelps didn't worry, having taken part in other relays and practicing harder on his starts than any team member at training camp.

The next day Phelps and Crocker passed through to the finals of the 100 butterfly. The final, five hours later, would be Phelps's seventeenth race at the Olympics. Crocker took the lead from the start in the tight race.

But Phelps beat Crocker with his final stroke, finishing a fraction of a second faster. He'd won the gold medal and a spot on the U.S. medley relay team. While Phelps wouldn't go home with seven gold medals, or Speedo's $1 million bonus, he had won five gold medals, and two bronze medals. Now he looked ahead to the medley relay and a chance at his sixth gold medal.

Crocker won the silver medal but it was a crushing defeat. He had hoped to earn three gold medals and would now go home without one. Although Phelps won a spot on the team by swimming in the preliminaries he gave up his spot on the relay team so Crocker could swim in his place. Phelps's selfless decision shocked the world and left Crocker speechless.

Michael and Diana Munz (right) cheer for the U.S. Olympic swim team from the stands. (*Courtesy of AP Images/Mark Baker*)

"This is a decision that I chose," Phelps said. "We came in as a team; we will leave as a team. I will be in the stands cheering." Remembering his sister Whitney's experience, he added, "It's one thing to train your hardest, be at your best and finish second. It's another to train your hardest and have injury or illness keep you from making your best attempt."

On the final day of Olympic swimming Phelps slept in. After getting up, he found a McDonalds that prepared him a special order, an entire bag full of Egg McMuffins. He posed for a photo with the kids working

Michael talks with McDonald's employees at the 2004 Olympic games. *(Courtesy of Getty Images)*

the counter. That evening he returned to the Olympic Aquatic Center and watched and cheered as the U.S. relay team won the gold medal and lowered the world record by an entire second. Although Phelps didn't swim in the event, he had qualified in the preliminaries so he too received a gold medal.

Phelps had earned six gold and two bronze medals. He was the first Olympian to win eight medals since gymnast Aleksandr Dityatin, at the 1980 Olympics in Moscow.

After Phelps won his last medal he planned one final dinner at a café in the *Plaka* with his family. A security officer advised him against it though, suggesting Phelps remain in the Olympic Village for his own safety. Frustrated, he stood on his balcony, calling friends and family on his cell phone. During the games he had kept his medals tucked in his clothes in a bag under his bed, until Bowman moved them to a safe deposit box in Athens. Now he thought about the dedication it took to win them.

Soon Phelps checked out of the Olympic Village and into a state room, courtesy of *Sports Illustrated,* on a cruise ship. Over the next few days he watched Olympic soccer and baseball, promoted his sponsors, and gave interviews. In the week after his races he received five hundred text messages on his cell

The 2004 Olympics closing ceremony

phone, some of them greetings, others interview requests.

On Sunday August 29 the 2004 Olympics closed underneath a full moon that lit the Athens sky. Although Phelps was weary, even before these games ended, he started thinking about the next ones.

five

In Too Deep

After the Olympic Games, Phelps had little time for rest. For his homecoming in Baltimore the town planned a celebration they called Phelpstival. The *Baltimore Sun* held a contest to find the best nickname for their hero: entries included "Phast Phish," "Phantom of the Aqua," and "Greece Lightning." Nearly 10,000 people lined the streets of Baltimore, clutching Wheaties cereal boxes, Speedos, and other items for Phelps to sign. Four fans painted the letters *M-I-K-E* on their stomachs. Even a local funeral home joined the businesses draping their windows with signs of congratulations.

Meadowbrook, Phelps's home pool in Baltimore, also received recognition. "People call our swim

Michael waves to the crowd at his homecoming Phelpstival in Baltimore, Maryland. *(Courtesy of AP Images/Matthew S. Gunby)*

school," said Bowman, and Phelps is "like a character in the Harry Potter books, 'He whose name cannot be spoken.'"

Soon Phelps flew to Orlando, Florida and boarded a tour bus for a monthlong cross-country tour. He, Crocker, and Krayzelburg traveled the country in style. The bus, formerly belonging to magician David Copperfield, slept twelve and had a microwave and large television screen, which the swimmers used for video games. For one of the first times Phelps wasn't with his mother and coach.

As part of the *Swim with the Stars* tour, Phelps conducted swim camps for children. *(Courtesy of AP Images)*

"No Mom, and no Bob," Phelps said. "Being away from Bob was actually weirder. When I'm at a meet, I really don't get to see my mom, but from the time I was twelve, I had never spent more than forty-eight hours away from Bob."

The tour, called *Swim with the Stars,* began at Disneyworld in Florida and ended at Disneyland in California. Across 7,000 miles and fifteen pools, the three Olympians signed autographs, conducted camps for swimmers of all ages, raced against each

other, took turns swimming as anchors on kids' relay teams, and swam relays with kids riding on their backs.

In Seattle, Washington students greeted the bus with the sign "Michael made History x Eight." During question and answer sessions the Olympians fielded questions ranging from their race times and tactics to their favorite ice cream flavors and pets. The three swimmers wanted to create more excitement about swimming and encourage more children to take up the sport.

"Swimming's done so much for me, more than I can give back to it, and I just want them to feel some part of what I feel," Phelps said. "On my crappiest day, when I'm tired or jet-lagged, I jump in that water and just something happens that I can't even put into words. I feel better and stronger, all the soreness goes, and I'm me again, a hundred percent back."

One day during the tour he felt a sharp pain on his lower right side. It flared up during the start of a race and Phelps gingerly emerged from the pool. Always sensitive to back pain he worried though the pain subsided. Physical therapists assumed the condition was the result of six weeks without training and a month of sitting on a bus.

The tour ended on October 5, and as Phelps traveled to the airport with his mother and coach they realized their car was being followed. At the airport two men and a woman emerged from the other car and tried to force their way into Phelps's car. One of the men was the limousine driver who had stalked Phelps before. Bowman confronted the man. Although security guards detained him the incident made everyone anxious.

Phelps's worries increased when his back tightened up following another race. After examining an image of Phelps's back, an orthopedic surgeon found damage to two of the vertebra in his lower back. Common among young athletes, the injury was due to repetitive hyperextension. Phelps remembered his sister Whitney's career-ending back problems. Now doctors prescribed caution and limited his training to twenty minutes of freestyle each day, along with wearing a back brace. Phelps had trouble backing off the training he had done every day for the last twelve years. He was depressed, scared, and bored.

In the fall of 2004, Phelps began attending the University of Michigan, where Bowman had taken a coaching job. Bowman hoped to make Ann Arbor the swimming capital of the United States. He coached a handful of swimmers who combined had won nineteen Olympic medals. Bowman custom ordered a clock to

A football game at Michigan Stadium. Michael entered the University of Michigan in the fall of 2004.

count down in tenths of seconds the time until the 2008 Olympics in Beijing, China.

Despite Phelps's achievements, sponsors, television commercials, and fame, he was like other college freshman leaving home for the first time. He moved into an apartment but fumbled his way through his first few months. He filled the dishwasher with hand soap which foamed up and covered his carpet with soapy bubbles. When his smoke alarm randomly kept going off he called Bowman, who told him to change the batteries. Phelps also ate his cereal out of Gatorade bottles because he kept forgetting to buy bowls.

As a professional athlete Phelps was ineligible to compete in college, but he acted as a volunteer assistant coach for the varsity team, the Wolverines. He also tried to adjust to his new environment, balancing classes, training, and life on his own. Upset and frustrated, the Olympian worried about fitting in with the other students and talked to his coach.

"I had to tell him," Bowman said, "'Well, Michael, you don't really fit in anywhere, but you will.'"

An introductory speech class highlighted Phelps's differences. The professor asked each student to bring in an item they were proud of and talk about themselves for five minutes. For his college show-and-tell Phelps brought in one of his gold medals. When asked which race it was from, Phelps admitted he didn't know. Written on the medal were the words *200 meters*, but the rest was written in Greek; it could be the 200 butterfly or the 200 IM.

Phelps held what seemed like the weight of the world's expectations on his shoulders, and he was only nineteen. Although he sometimes wanted to hide as a public figure, he couldn't. On November 4, he drank beer at a party and drove his car through a stop sign in front of a policeman. The officer charged

Michael (second from top right) leaves court after pleading guilty to drunken driving charges. *(Courtesy of AP Images/Chris Gardner)*

him with driving under the influence of alcohol and drinking under the age of twenty-one. Within days he admitted his mistake publicly and profusely, telephoning reporters and news services. Ordered to pay fines and court costs, Phelps fulfilled his community service by speaking out at local schools against drinking and driving.

"I made a serious mistake, and I needed to man up to what I had done," Phelps said. "For eight years my life had been so structured. I had little or no freedom. When I finally got some, I grabbed too much."

Phelps spent the next months stewing in frustration and embarrassment. On the heels of his drinking offense he received bad news. On December 6, doctors saw a stress fracture on a second image of his back. Phelps had three options: stop training for six months; train through the pain and risk further problems; or have his back surgically repaired with screws and a bone graft, facing a recovery time and three months without any swimming. He got a second opinion from the U.S. Olympic team's physician. After studying Phelp's history the physician suggested that Phelps resume training, but decrease his workload.

"When it was suggested that Michael take six months off, it might as well have been a death sentence for him," Bowman said. "We were all walking around like he was made of eggshells, wondering if he'll be able to move eight years down the road, but the injuries to his back were so minute and . . . after a few days of inactivity . . . Michael became symptom-free."

Phelps straightened out other aspects of his life. After his humbling experiences he'd thought about leaving the University of Michigan. Matters had come to a head when Phelps lived with Bowman during November and December before moving into the townhouse in Ann Arbor he planned to buy. Spending entire days together in the pool and at home frayed their nerves. When Bowman asked Phelps if he was eating and sleeping enough Phelps exploded. After telling his coach to stop treating him like a child, Phelps walked out, saying he was going back to Baltimore.

After Phelps talked to his mother and mulled his situation for a few hours he went to the pool, where he often sorted life out. Phelps decided to stay and days later signed the contract to buy the four-story townhouse. He moved in his belongings, along with his XBox, and slept on a borrowed air mattress, putting some much-needed space between him and his coach.

Phelps gradually adjusted to college life. He took a light course load, intending to major in sports marketing or sports management and got an *M,* for Michigan,

An English bulldog

tattooed on his left hip, to balance the Olympic rings on his right. Phelps found comfortable haunts, similar to Pete's Grille. He discovered cheeseburger subs, buffalo enchiladas, and waffle cones filled with vanilla ice cream and bits of Butterfinger candy bars. Finally, he got himself a dog—an English bulldog named Herman.

When Phelps appeared in a competition to qualify for the 2005 World Championships he appeared to be back in form. According to his physician he'd made his usual superhuman recovery. He won the 200 IM, caught Crocker in the 100 butterfly, and upset Jason Lezak in the 100 freestyle. But he still faced difficulties. After a third-place finish in one race his lactate reading was so high Bowman refused to tell him the count. Now that Phelps had settled into college life he began to turn his attention fully back to the sport he loved.

six

Till I Collapse

U nlike typical college students who budgeted time for exams and papers, Phelps had to balance his sponsors too. After the Olympics they clamored for him to appear. Although he'd worried about his sponsors dropping him after his drinking and driving arrest, they didn't. In March of 2005 he signed a deal with Matsunichi, an electronics company in Hong Kong that manufactured watches and MP3 players. One of the most lucrative sponsorship deals for an Olympic athlete, Phelps would earn $1 million annually through 2008.

Later Phelps traveled to Hong Kong for a promotional tour. On his five-day trip he kept an online diary for USA Swimming and met with young Chinese swimmers who called him the Flying Fish. After Phelps took in the city's neon lights and skyscrapers, he dined on a lavish traditional dinner of twelve dishes, including eel gills, goose livers, duck eggs, jellyfish heads, a salad of flower petals, and Peking duck, which he discovered he liked.

Two days later, exactly a year since he'd won his first gold medal in Athens, Phelps toured the National Aquatics Center that would host Olympic swimming in 2008. On his last full day in China, he walked along the Great Wall. Seldom before had he been able to tour the sites around the world where he raced.

In July of 2005, just a few months after his twentieth birthday, Phelps competed in the World Championships in Montreal, Canada. It was his first international competition since Athens, and he had a daunting schedule. His performance was inconsistent. In his first individual race, the 400 freestyle, he didn't advance to the finals. Then he helped the American team win the 400 freestyle relay. Two nights later Phelps won the 200 freestyle, which made his first loss puzzling.

The following day he finished seventh in the final of the 100 freestyle, but dominated the 200 IM an hour later. Next he became the youngest member on the victorious 800 freestyle relay then lost the 100 butterfly to Crocker.

Michael warms up before a promotional swimming event in Hong Kong.
(Courtesy of AP Images/Kin Cheung)

The new experience caused many to wonder whether Michael Phelps's career was cooling off. Although he walked away from the event with five golds and one silver, he fell short of his own standards. Only a handful of swimmers in the world could understand being disappointed at such a performance.

"I'm not where I want to be right now," said Phelps. "This world championship has sort of been a big wake-up call. It hasn't been a normal year for me. The only thing I can do is use this as motivation."

In just one year Phelps had competed in the Olympics, toured the United States, started college, and faced a potentially career-ending medical crisis. He'd also had to deal with a public crisis, damaging his image with his drunken driving offense. Phelps and Bowman sat down and planned to shift priorities. They decided he needed to spend more time in the pool and less plugging ads for his sponsors.

"Each year between Sydney and Athens, one-thousand decisions were made, and 999 of them were made correctly," Phelps said. "This past year, maybe six-hundred out of one-thousand were the right call. Decisions were made that were not going to improve my swimming. That's why I'm where I am in the swim world."

Although he switched his focus, Phelps remained dedicated to spreading his passion for swimming. In late September, *Unfiltered*, the first behind-the-scenes documentary on swimming, premiered. The seventy-five minute film followed friends and rivals Michael Phelps and Ian Crocker in the moments leading up to the World Championships. The documentary featured home videos, photos, personal insights, and interviews with coaches, family, and friends.

Phelps and Bowman also put together a video they titled *Personal Best*. The video offered instruction

The Phelps family, (from left to right) Whitney, Hilary, Debbie, and Michael, prepares to watch the world premiere of *Unfiltered*. *(Courtesy of Getty Images)*

on the butterfly, showing drills Phelps used to work on his stroke and kick. The filmmakers captured photos of Phelps at different angles in the water. Bowman interviewed Phelps about his swimming and preparation, asking if he had a special diet.

"My mom makes sure I eat enough fruits and vegetables," said Phelps. "I just want to cram in what I can."

In 2006, he and his mother attended the Winter Olympics. In Torino, Italy Phelps watched more athletes chase their Olympic dreams. He vowed to continue visiting the Aquatic Center in Beijing, where in less than two years he would attempt to match his previous record.

In 2007, Phelps moved on to the World Championships in Melbourne, Australia, attempting to improve his performance. He succeeded against the best swimmers in the world. He captured seven gold medals and broke five world records between March 25 and April 1.

Phelps had gone alone to the events in Australia, leaving Bowman behind in the U.S. for a Wolverines meet. Despite the massive amounts of time they spent together, and their history of conflicts, the two had a joking relationship. "Bob texted me the other day and asked if I missed him," Phelps said. "I typed back, 'Ummm . . . not really.'"

The sometime turbulent but deeply bonded relationship between Phelps and Bowman has helped Phelps become the world's greatest swimmer. He has eight Olympic medals and has set world records thirteen times. He also holds nineteen American records and twenty-seven titles from the U.S. Nationals. He is a ten-time World Champion, has been named U.S. Swimmer of the Year three times,

and was crowned Outstanding Male Athlete of the Year in 2004.

As the 2008 Summer Olympics in Beijing approached, many wondered if Phelps could repeat his Olympic performance from 2004.

"Now if he can do in Beijing the same thing he did in Athens he'd be the first guy to do it twice," said longtime Olympics announcer Jim Lampley. "Then you have to put that phrase 'greatest of all time' into the thought process."

Swimming legend Mark Spitz also wondered about Phelps's chances of beating his record.

"Somebody asked me what I would think if Michael won seven gold medals, and I said, 'It would be like the second man on the moon,'" Spitz said. "Then [the interviewer] asked 'What if he wins eight?' and I said 'First man on Mars.'"

"I know what I want to do," Phelps said. "If it happens, great. If I become the most decorated Olympian, I do. I'm going through life, doing something I love."

In a locker room at the University of Michigan, a clock ticked off tenths of seconds, as the 2008 Olympics approached. The world awaited Michael Phelps's next showdown with the world's best swimmers.

seven

The Greatest

A s 2008 began, Michael Phelps's focus, as well as the focus of much of the sporting world, was on the 2008 Olympics in Beijing, the capital city of the People's Republic of China.

Phelps was entered in eight events, including three relays. This meant he'd have to depend on his teammates to help him win the coveted eight gold medals. With the two gold medals he had won in Sydney in 2004, this would allow him to win more gold medals than anyone in history—if he went undefeated in all eight events.

Most of the people watching the Olympics were not aware of how close Phelps had come to losing his

dream before the events even began. The previous October he had slipped on the ice in Michigan and broken his wrist. The accident had hampered his practice schedule and could have altered his stroke. But nothing was going to stop Phelps from his chance to win the most golds in a single Olympics ever, and by August his wrist was as good as new.

When he arrived in Beijing, Phelps repeated to reporters that he wanted to win eight golds. He also had another goal. "I wanted to do something nobody ever did," he told the *New York Times*. "This goes hand in hand with my goal of changing swimming." One of his goals in becoming a swimming superstar, he repeated often, was to make swimming a more popular sport, especially among children. He knew how the sport had helped him as a youth when his family was going through rough times. He was convinced swimming could help other young people.

The pressure was intense. Phelps had to find time to continue his training, eat well, and get plenty of rest. He had also agreed to submit to drug testing after each event so there would be no rumors that he had used muscle-enhancing drugs. Several sports have been rocked over the previous few years by revelations that some of the best players had taken steroids and other drugs that gave them an unfair

Phelps shares his Olympic experience with children during a visit to the Boys and Girls Club of Burbank, in Burbank, California. *(Courtesy of AP Images)*

advantage. Phelps was determined that no one could say that about him.

Phelps's first event was the 400-meter individual medley, always one of his strongest events. He broke his own world record in his preliminary swim. In the

finals he broke the record again and won his first gold of the 2008 games.

The next event would turn out to be one of the most exciting of the entire Olympics—and not because of Phelps.

Phelps competing in the 400-meter individual medley. *(Courtesy of AP Images)*

The entire team knew the 4 X 100 freestyle relay was going to be one of its biggest challenges. Phelps himself was much better in 200 and 400 meter events. In addition, the French team, which was heavily favored, had Alain Bernard, who had a few months earlier broken the world record for the 100-meter freestyle.

Phelps swam the first leg and held his own. The U.S. team was in a solid second place. By the last leg, that looked like where it would end up. When American Jason Lezak, who was swimming the final leg, went into the water he was at least a body length and a half behind Bernard—an almost unbridgeable distance by the standards of such high-quality swimmers.

On the last 50 meters, however, Lezak began gaining on the French superstar. Incredibly, in the last second, Lezak pushed past Bernard and touched the wall a fraction of a second before. He swam an almost miraculous swim and pulled it out for himself and his teammates. Phelps burst out with a yell and a cheer that was flashed around the world.

Phelps's next race was another of his favorite events. He held the record in the 200-meter freestyle. In the finals of this event he broke his own record. He finished almost two seconds in front of the silver medal winner.

Phelps (right) cheers after Lezak beat out French swimmer Bernard to win the gold for the U.S. men's 4 X 100 freestyle relay team. *(Courtesy of AP Images/Thomas Kienzle)*

Phelps kept up his grueling schedule the next day. He had finals in two events. He won another gold in the 200-meter butterfly, setting another world record. During this swim his goggles slipped and filled up with water. He couldn't see where he was going the last 100 meters. This is when his hard work paid off: he was experienced enough to have his count of strokes right and knew when he was at the wall to make his turn and his finish.

Phelps was not able to rest between events because he had to have his drug test completed. Less than an hour later he was in the water to swim the first leg of the 4 X 200 freestyle relay. The American team won this relay handily, becoming the first team to win the event in less than seven minutes.

After the two-event day, Phelps had a day to rest. The break could not have come at a better time. When he came back on August 16 he faced his biggest obstacle to winning the eight gold medals.

The 100-meter butterfly was the first individual event that he did not hold the world record in before the games began. His old American competitor Ian Crocker still held that record.

His principal challenger was Milorad Čavić of Serbia. This time, the finishing time was even closer than the 4 X 100 freestyle relay. Most observers thought Čavić

had won the event, but when the times appeared on the scoreboard Michael had won. The margin was 1/100 of a second.

Although Čavić admitted that Phelps had won, the Serbian coaches filed a protest. The underwater film of the final second confirmed that Phelps had used his

Phelps reacts after beating Milorad Čavić by 1/100 of a second to win his seventh gold medal of the 2008 games. *(Courtesy of AP Images/Petr David Josek)*

strong finish to push past Čavić by a fingertip. Later, Čavić told reporters that he had made a mistake at the very end and miscounted, which reduced his speed too soon and left Phelps an opportunity he get his finger on the stop clock first.

This stunning victory gave Phelps his seventh gold medal, tying Mark Spitz's 1972 record. His final event was the 4 X 100 medley relay. Phelps swam the butterfly leg, the third of the four. When he entered the water the Americans were in third place. When he finished the Americans were in the lead by one-half of a second. Jason Lezak, again swimming the last leg of a critical relay, held onto the lead and the U.S. swim team had another gold medal.

At the end of the event Phelps managed to keep his cool long enough to talk to reporters. Despite his historical achievement, he was modest. "Records are always made to be broken no matter what they are," he told CNN, "anybody can do anything that they set their mind to."

He was also careful to let it be known that although he had set a new Olympic precedent, he still had deep respect for Mark Spitz. "What he did was and still is an amazing feat, and will always be an amazing accomplishment for the swimming world and also the Olympics," Phelps said of Spitz. "I've said it all along,

Phelps celebrates winning his eighth gold medal after the men's 4x100-meter medley relay final. *(Courtesy of (AP Images/David J. Phillip)*

I want to be the first Michael Phelps, not a second Mark Spitz."

The next day, before he left Beijing, Michael got a call from President George W. Bush, who was in China for the Olympics. The entire United States was proud of him, the president said. He also invited him

Phelps hugs his mother Debbie, left, after the medal ceremony for the men's 4x100-meter medley relay final. *(Courtesy of AP Images/Itsuo Inouye)*

to meet with him at the White House. A story also began circulating that the president's daughter Jenna, who had recently broken up with her boyfriend, was intrigued and wanted to meet Phelps. It was even joked that the president was trying to set up Phelps with his daughter.

When the swimming part of the Olympics was over Phelps took his traditional trip to McDonalds and enjoyed escaping the intense training regiment for a few days. But he knew his life had changed forever.

When reporters asked him what the future held for Michael Phelps he repeated that he wanted to be an ambassador for swimming. One of his goals is to spread the word of what a great and beneficial sport it is. He also wants to work to have more pools built so children from poorer neighborhoods will have the same opportunity he had.

Phelps also has more private goals. He is in high demand to endorse products and to do advertisements. He will probably make millions of dollars over the next few years. He also announced plans to write a book about his experiences as a swimmer and to carry on his goal of advancing the sport.

Phelps's deadpan sense of humor and genuine modesty has also made him a much sought after guest on television shows. He has appeared on a variety of TV programs, including the late night talk show *Jimmy Kimmel Live*, and as a presenter at the *2008 MTV Video Music Awards*. He also hosted the 2008 season premiere of the famous show *Saturday Night Live*.

After his stunning victories in Beijing, Phelps was often asked if he would participate in the 2012 Olympics, in London. Phelps responded that he intended to do so. If he does, it will surely only add to his Olympic legacy. Currently, he has fourteen medals; if he competes in London, he could become the most medaled Olympian ever, besting Larissa Latynina, a Soviet gymnast who competed in 1956, 1960, and 1964, and holds eighteen medals, nine of which are gold.

Michael Phelps's life will continue to be a mixture of hard work and fun. So far he has managed to maintain a healthy balance, and when he has failed to do so, he has worked to fix the problem, learn his lesson, and continue. His perseverance and ability to learn from both his mistakes and successes will continue to serve him well as he looks forward to years of swimming.

Phelps (right) performing on a *Saturday Night Live* skit with other cast members. *(Courtesy of Dana Edelson/NBCU Photo Bank/AP Images)*

PHELPS'S 2008 GOLD MEDAL WINS

Event	Results	Time
400 m individual medley	World Record	4:03.84[54]
4 x 100 m freestyle relay	World Record	3:08.24[55]
200 m freestyle	World Record	1:42.96[56]
200 m butterfly	World Record	1:52.03[57]
4 x 200 m freestyle relay	World Record	6:58.56[57]
200 m individual medley	World Record	1:54.23[58]
100 m butterfly	Olympic Record	50.58[59]
4 x 100 m medley relay	World Record	3:29.34[60]

Timeline

1985   Born on June 30 in Baltimore, Maryland.

1992   Takes his first swimming lesson.

1994   Parents, Debbie and Fred Phelps, divorce.

1996   Begins working with coach Bob Bowman.

2000   Qualifies for the Olympic Games in Sydney,
        Australia, becoming the youngest male swimmer
        on a U.S. Olympic team in sixty-eight years;
        finishes fifth in the 200-meter butterfly in Sydney.

2001   Becomes the youngest male swimmer ever to break
        a world record; in Japan lowers his own record
        and wins his first world title; forfeits his amateur
        status to turn professional.

2003   Becomes the first male to win titles in three of the
        four different strokes at a national championship
        meet; graduates from Towson High School; breaks
        five world records at the World Championships
        in Barcelona, Spain.

2004   Qualifies to swim six individual events in the
        2004 Olympic Games in Athens, Greece, where
        he wins six gold and two bronze medals; takes a
        post-Olympic tour called *Swim with the Stars*;

begins attending the University of Michigan; diagnosed with a stress fracture in his back.

2005   Wins six medals at the World Championships in Montreal, Canada; stars in the documentary *Unfiltered* with fellow swimmer Ian Crocker.

2006   Finishes first in six of seven races at the U.S. Nationals in California; sets three world records at the Pan Pacific games.

2007   Becomes a seven-time gold medalist at the World Championships in Australia where he breaks five world records.

2008   Swims in Beijing Olympics, wins gold medals in eight events, setting record for most gold wins in a single Olympic Games.

Sources

CHAPTER ONE: Born to Swim

p. 11, "I'm cold . . ." Michael Phelps and Brian Cazeneuve, *Michael Phelps: Beneath the Surface* (Champaign, IL: Sports Publishing, 2005), 16.

p. 12, "They don't care . . ." Paul McMullen, *Amazing Pace* (New York: Rodale Books, 2006), 4.

p. 18, "One, two, three . . ." Phelps and Cazeneuve, *Michael Phelps: Beneath the Surface, 22.*

p. 19, "focus on anything . . ." Paul Solotaroff, "How Do You Improve on Greatest Ever?" *Men's Journal,* July 2007, 84.

p. 20, "I can almost . . ." McMullen, *Amazing Pace,* 10.

p. 21, "Little Phelps," Ibid, 8.

p. 22, "He'd seen me . . ." Solotaroff, "How Do You Improve on Greatest Ever?" 148.

p. 23, "Beware of Bob," Phelps and Cazeneuve,

Michael Phelps:Beneath the Surface, 28.

p. 25, "The thing that . . ." McMullen, *Amazing Pace,* 22.

CHAPTER TWO: The Land Down Under

p. 29, "Michael, if you're . . ." Phelps and Cazeneuve,
   Michael Phelps: Beneath the Surface, 53.

p. 29, "There wasn't much . . ." Ibid, 43.

p. 30, "Micheal is not . . ." Ibid, 52.

p. 31, "There's the one . . ." Ibid, 108-109.

p. 33, "Shaving a guy's . . ." Ibid, 189.

p. 35, "If I'm third . . ." Ibid, 69.

p. 37, "Hello, America . . ." Ibid, 73.

p. 44, "Nobody has ever . . ." Ibid, 88.

p. 44, "I just started . . ." Ibid, 89.

p. 46, "It was an . . ." Ibid, 107.

p. 46, "You always give . . ." McMullen, *Amazing Pace,*
   146.

CHAPTER THREE: The Human Shark

p. 51, "You want to . . ." Phelps and Cazeneuve, *Michael
   Phelps: Beneath the Surface,* 173.

p. 53, "We've got Ian . . ." Ibid, 133.

p. 53, "Sometimes you feel . . ." Ibid, 5.

p. 55, "Dog?" Ibid, 141.

p. 55, "2 Dogs?" Ibid, 142.

p. 55, "What's this about . . ." McMullen, *Amazing
   Pace,* 25.

p. 56, "3 Dogs?" Phelps and Cazeneuve, *Michael
   Phelps: Beneath the Surface,* 142.

p. 56, "4 Dogs?" Ibid, 142.

p. 57, "The first thing . . ." Ibid, 143.

p. 57, "El Nuevo Spitz . . ." McMullen, *Amazing Pace,* 16.

p. 58, "You need to . . ." Phelps and Cazeneuve, *Michael Phelps: Beneath the Surface,* 144.

p. 58, *"Phelps es Humano,"* Ibid., 145.

p. 58, "I had been . . ." McMullen, *Amazing Pace,* 27.

p. 58, "5 Dogs?" Phelps and Cazeneuve, *Michael Phelps: Beneath the Surface,* 145.

p. 62, "One" McMullen, *Amazing Pace,* 80.

p. 65, "I'll be over . . ." Phelps and Cazeneuve, *Michael Phelps: Beneath the Surface,* 182.

CHAPTER FOUR: The Ancient Games

p. 70, "Think about it . . ." McMullen, *Amazing Pace,* 109.

p. 71, "If they manage . . ." Ibid, 100.

p. 71, "A pool is . . ." Ibid, 111.

p. 75, "Mom, look what . . ." Ibid, 180.

p. 76, "The world has . . ." Phelps and Cazeneuve, *Michael Phelps: Beneath the Surface,* 205.

p. 78, "We owned that . . ." Ibid, 211.

p. 78, "I like to . . ." McMullen, *Amazing Pace,* 192.

p. 78, "Michael doesn't let . . ." *Unfiltered: The Story Behind the Rivalry,* DVD, directed by Brian Edelman, Sean Keegan and Luke Korver (McLean, Virginia: Cross Borders Productions, 2005).

p. 81, "This is a . . ." Eric Adelson, "Phelps Done," *ESPN,* August 20, 2004.

p. 81, "It's one thing . . ." Phelps and Cazeneuve, *Michael Phelps: Beneath the Surface,* 218.

CHAPTER FIVE: In Too Deep

p. 84-85, "People call our . . ." McMullen, *Amazing Pace,*
38.

p. 86, "No Mom and. . ." Ibid, 209.

p. 87, "Michael made history . . ." Jim Moore, "Go 2
Guy: Swim Stars Make Quite a Splash," *Seattle
Post-Intelligencer,* September 28, 2004.

p. 87, "Swimming's done so . . ." Solotaroff, "How Do
You Improve on Greatest Ever?" 149.

p. 90, "I had to . . ." John Niyo, "Phelps is Adjusting to
Life Out of the Pool. But Eight-Time Olympic Medalist
No Longer Doubts His Move to Ann Arbor," *Detroit
News,* March 8, 2005.

p. 91, "I made a . . ." McMullen, *Amazing Pace,* 212.

p. 92, "When it was . . ." Ibid, 214.

CHAPTER SIX: Till I Collapse

p. 97, "I'm not where . . ." McMullen, *Amazing
Pace*, 221.

p. 98, "Each year between. . ." Ibid, 204.

p. 99, "My mom makes . . ." Phelps and Cazeneuve, *Michael
Phelps: Beneath the Surface,* 103.

p. 100, "Bob texted me . . ." Beth Harris, "Phelps on the
Brink of Two Year Odyssey," Associated Press, January,
13, 2007, washingtonpost.com, http://www.
washingtonpost.com/wp-dyn/content/article/2007/01/12/
AR2007011201759.html.

p. 101, "Now if he . . ." Childs Walker, "None Better,"
Baltimore Sun, April 6, 2007.

p. 101, "Somebody asked me . . ." David Barron, "When
Michael Phelps Hits the Pool at the Beijing Olympics,

He'll be Chasing Mark Spitz's 1972 Record of 7 Golds in 7 Events," *Houston Chronicle,* August, 10, 2007, 13.

p. 101, "I know what . . ." McMullen, *Amazing Pace,* 226.

CHAPTER SEVEN: The Greatest

p. xx, "I wanted to do something . . ." Karen Crouse. "Phelps Epic Journey Ends in Perfection," *New York Times*, August 17, 2008.

p. xx, "Records are always made . . ." "Phelps wins historic eight gold medal," *CNN.com*, August 18, 2008.

p. xx, "What he did was and . . ." Ibid.

Bibliography

Abrahamson, Alan. "Can Phelps Be the Best? Next Two
    Years Will Tell." NBC Sports, January 12, 2007.
    http://www.NBCSports.com (accessed July
    9, 2007)

Adelson, Eric. "Phelps Done." *ESPN,* August 20, 2004.

Barnas, Jo-ann. "Phelps Finds Rhythm, Comfort in Ann
    Arbor." *Detroit Free Press,* May 19, 2006.

Crouse, Karen. "Phelps' Epic Journey Ends in Perfection."
    New York Times, August 17, 2008.

Harris, Beth. "Phelps on the Brink of Two Year Odyssey."
    Associated Press, January 13, 2007. website. http://www.
    michaelphelps.com (accessed July 10, 2007)

McMullen, Paul. *Amazing Pace.* New York: Rodale
    Books, 2006.

Moore, Jim. "Go 2 Guy: Swim Stars Make Quite a Splash."
    Seattle Post-Intelligencer, September 28, 2004.

Niyo, John. "Phelps is Adjusting to Life Out of the Pool.
    But Eight-Time Olympic Medalist No Longer Doubts

His Move to Ann Arbor." *Detroit News,* March
8, 2005.

Phelps, Michael, and Brian Cazeneuve. *Michael Phelps:
Beneath the Surface.* Champaign, IL: Sports Publishing,
2005.

Phelps, Michael, and Ian Crocker. *Unfiltered: The Story
Behind the Rivalry.* McLean, Virginia: Octagon, 2005.

"Records are always made to be broken." *CNN.com*
August 18, 2008.

Shipley, Amy. "Emerging from Troubled Water After
Mistakes, Phelps Says He is Out to Prove He has
Matured." *Washington Post,* August 1, 2006.

Walker, Childs. "None Better." *Baltimore Sun,* April 6, 2007.

Zuehlke, Jeffrey. *Michael Phelps.* Minneapolis, MN:
Lerner Publishing, 2005.

Web sites

http://michaelphelps.com
Michael Phelps's official site. It includes his biography, pictures, articles, recent news about him, links to other swimming sites, and contact information for asking Phelps questions.

http://usaswimming.org
This is the USA Olympic Training Center's Web site. It covers swimming101, health, nutrition, swimming rules and tips, and information about the Olympic swim team members.

http://www.en.beijing2008.com
Coverage of the 2008 Beijing Olympics can be found on this site. It offers a peek at the newly built sports venues, descriptions of the summer sports, and information about the history of the Olympics, the torch, and the culture and excitement surrounding the world event.

Index